The Big

12

My Personal Confidence-Building
Principles for Achieving Total Success

JESSE DUPLANTIS

Tulsa, OK

10 9 8 7 6 5 4 3 2 1   17 18 19 20

The Big 12
Copyright © 2017 by Jesse Duplantis
Jesse Duplantis Ministries, Destrehan, LA 70047

ISBN: 978-1-68031-173-0

Published by Harrison House Publishers
Tulsa, OK 74145
www.harrisonhouse.com

Contents

INTRODUCTION 1

PRINCIPLE 1 3
Know What You Want—Be Clear and Shape Your Own Destiny

PRINCIPLE 2 9
*Use Those Lonely "Wilderness Times" to Get Clearer Focus
On Your Calling and Goals*

PRINCIPLE 3 15
*Do Not Seek Approval from People—Listen to God's "Still, Small
Voice"*

PRINCIPLE 4 23
*Is There Not a Cause? Passion is the Power That Creates Life and
Helps You Achieve Success*

PRINCIPLE 5 31
Don't Settle for the Land of Better—Aim to Dwell in the Land of Best

PRINCIPLE 6 39
Don't Judge Others—It Opens Up Your Life to Major Leaks

PRINCIPLE 7 45
Listening Will Help You to See Your Situation in New Ways

PRINCIPLE 8 51
Respect the Royalty in Yourself and Others

PRINCIPLE 9 57
*Always Keep Encouragement Close to Your Heart—It's the Oxygen
of the Soul*

PRINCIPLE 10 63
Always Be Generous—Take as Many to the Top with You as You Can

PRINCIPLE 11 71
Never, Never, Never Report the News—Make the News

PRINCIPLE 12 79
Never Waste Your Energy and Zeal on Projects That Don't Work

Introduction

Everywhere I go, I meet people who want success in their life. Believers, unbelievers, and people from all walks of life—all of us know instinctively that success beats failure, and we want to succeed.

I believe that God is a good God and He has given everyone in this world life for a purpose—to bring something into the world that was not here before, to do something that needs doing, and to succeed in shining a light that has never shone before.

That light is you. And this means that I believe YOU have the potential to succeed, no matter what anyone has said or done to try and stop you. You *are* a success going somewhere to succeed—and it's time for you to believe it.

People are always asking me how is it that I've succeeded in areas that others haven't—preachers, laymen, those in business and people from all sorts of different walks of life. The answer is very simple and the same to all of them: I've found some things that work!

In this book, I'm going to share with you "The Big 12"—a list of personal confidence-building principles that I use in my own life to achieve success in what God has called me to do. Some I've come up with entirely on my own and others are important principles I've learned along the way, but all of them have been instrumental in my life in some way.

They are in no particular order, so you can read them in the order you'd like, but I hope you find value in every single one because each one has mattered to me so much. I don't take any of them lightly—they are each deep down in my heart—and I consistently find myself using them whenever something new comes up that I know I'm supposed to do.

"The Big 12"—they've helped me not only achieve success, but stay grounded in God in the process, and now I hope they help you too! After all, God has things for you to say, experience, and do in this life—and I believe He wants you to succeed in doing them. So, are you ready? Let's go!

PRINCIPLE

1

Know What You Want—
Be Clear and Shape Your Own Destiny

God has given you many gifts. Some are completely unique to you. Some have been inherited and some you've learned to tap into from experiences you've had with others. Everything that you've been given, everything that you've learned up to this point in your life, is going to help you get what you want and accomplish God's plan for your life.

No matter what you want to succeed at in this life, I want you to know you've got what it takes. You've got what you need *inside* to do what God calls you to do. It's in you—right now. What's the catch? It's also in God and you need His presence daily in your life to really access what's inside of you. You need His Word daily too. It's how you gain wisdom without falling into every ditch in life.

Bottom line? You need God's help to succeed in fulfilling His plan for your life. Being connected and maintaining that connection to God is going to help you with every big long-range decision you make—as well as give you the strength, power, discipline and joy to make all those daily decisions that will ultimately get you where you want to be.

Determine right now that success is God's plan for you. I don't care what you're looking at right now. If you are breathing, God has a plan to help you reach higher heights than where you are right now. I don't care what anybody else says—God's Word says that your place is at the top, not the bottom. Your place is above, not beneath. You were created to be the head and not the tail—which means that God wants you to use your head so you don't live like you're being dragged around life by your tail!

Don't accept whatever comes in life. Realize that you *can* shape your own destiny and get *out* of tailspin living—and you can start now by using this first principle.

Know What You Want
And Keep Knowing It!

You gotta know what you want! You can be talented. You can be brilliant. You can have every gift in the world. But you can't be successful if you don't know what you want. To be successful, you must not only know what you want—but *keep* knowing it!

Life gets busy and it's tempting to shove your missions and goals aside. But, if you ever want to succeed in that area, you can't allow your mission, goal, or heart's desire to slide into a state of dormancy in your own mind.

How do you keep that from happening? You do what the Word says and stir it up! 2 Timothy 1:5-6 says it this way:

*"When I call to remembrance the unfeigned faith that is in thee, which dwelt first in thy grandmother Lois, and thy mother Eunice; and I am persuaded that in thee also. Wherefore I put thee in remembrance that thou **stir up the gift** of God, which is in thee by the putting on of my hands".*

Never let anyone tell you that you're not good enough or smart enough. Don't let anyone convince you that you don't have anything to give to society. All that "you're not this or that" is a lie.

Listen to what the Word says instead of the naysayers, and stir yourself up! Stir up the gift that God has given you—don't throw it in the corner because you are busy. You use your mind every day anyway. Give yourself permission to put the mission where it needs to be—front and center. Because, no matter what, your success begins with believing, not forgetting! Here's the next part of this principle:

Be Clear About Your Mission
What You Believe, You Must Become.
What You Believe, You Must Do.

I'm not talking about just wishing; I'm talking about the boldness to *possess* the mission/vision/goal or heart's desire— whatever it is. What is your mission right now? What do you want to do? What's God put on your heart that just keeps coming up for you?

To succeed at it, you're going to have to start choosing to have an active, forward-thinking way of living—not just thinking, but living! It takes clarity of thought to get anything done.

You see, if you are clear about your mission, your mission will come out of the vision/faith "world" of your heart and mind and into the seen world of reality. In other words, people will one day *see* your mission instead of just hearing about it. Talk is cheap. Results are everlasting and cannot be denied.

Take debt, for instance. I meet a lot of people who just want to get out from under the pressure of debt—if you hear them talk, that's their mission. Yet they keep buying more things on credit. They can't seem to tell themselves "no." Sometimes you have to tell yourself no *for the moment* in order to get what you really want *in the end*. Your mission is too important to be sidetracked.

So if your mission is to be debt-free, then you must give it all you've got to achieve it—this means, you have to *know* you want to be debt-free. Not wish. KNOW. When I say, be clear about your mission, I mean that you must know—inside and out—that you want the end result enough to do what you have to do to get it. The process of getting there is part of your success.

What happens when something comes up that you just "have to have" but would put you more in debt? You have to stir yourself up. Be clear about your mission in that moment. When you are clear about your mission, no matter what tempts your flesh, you aren't taking the bait because you don't want to go into more debt! You are fully persuaded, "I'm paying off the debt I have now. I'm not getting more of it! This thing I'm looking at isn't worth compromising what I really want, end of statement."

If healing or changes in your body or mind is your mission, then you must *talk* those things day in and day out by speaking what the Word of God says about healing and what you can do in Christ Jesus. Over and over—not just on Sunday or every once in a while.

To accomplish your mission, the Word regarding what you want must be foremost in your mind—and your mouth. You can't say you want health and then allow thoughts of "I'll never get healed" or "This will never change" to permeate your thought-life every day. That's being double-minded, and you won't reach your goal or get what you want thinking or talking like that—and especially not doing the opposite of what you want.

Your mission must be clear: healing! Changes in your body! Health! Strength! Fitness! Whatever it is. So you can't do things that are directly against your mission if you want success. You have to decide that the process of getting to your mission is part of your success.

God told Joshua that if he wanted to be successful, he had to meditate on the Word day and night and observe to do what it said (Joshua 1:8). Don't give up on a great mission due to a temporary distraction. Know what you want. Stir it up. Keep meditating on the Word. Do what you have in your heart.

If God said you could be blessed—the lender and not the borrower—it's doable. If Jesus said by His stripes you would be able to gain healing for your body or mind, then it's doable. Use the Word and pursue your mission. Keep what God says on your lips.

Refuse Distraction

Your mission must be clearer to you than to anyone else.

You see, when you are clear about your mission, you begin to shape your own destiny. When Jerusalem lay in waste, Nehemiah spurred on the rebuilding when he said, *"Ye see the distress that we are in, how Jerusalem lieth waste, and the gates thereof are burned with fire:* **come, and let us build** *up the wall of Jerusalem, that we be no more a reproach…* **the God of Heaven, He will prosper us;** *therefore we His servants will* **arise and build**" (Nehemiah 2:17-20).

The walls of the city were very important for the people's security in life. It was Nehemiah's mission and destiny to build back that wall—and it was a mission he was clear about. He believed it more than anybody else and his conviction to do it ignited a fire within others to see that mission accomplished.

If you read further on, you find out that many people tried to distract Nehemiah from his mission, but he refused to be distracted. That's a lesson. NEVER let someone distract you from your own mission and destiny in life.

You getting results is more important than taking time with petty things, whether they are coming from your own mind or somebody else's mouth! Let that go, keep your mission clear, and keep on moving forward.

PRINCIPLE
2

Use Those Lonely "Wilderness Times" To Get Clearer Focus On Your Calling and Goals

This principle is about how I handle the lonely times in my life—those times when things don't seem to be going the way they are supposed to be going. I like to call them my "wilderness times."

I could wallow in the despondency that lonely times always try to bring, but I've always found that it does nothing for me, and never gets me any closer to achieving anything good. I have found that it is much better to just have faith in God—to stir up the gift inside, look to His Word, and find the ambition to continue moving forward in His plan.

So, when going through "the wilderness," this is the principle to use: Lonely times (wilderness times) in life help you to get clearer about your calling and your goals.

What, When, Where, and How

Saint Paul experienced what I call "the silent years" in his life and ministry (Galatians 1:15-24). These were times when he moved forward in God's plan but without very much support from the other apostles. He was moving ahead through what seemed like some pretty lonely times.

It's possible that you may be in this phase of your life now. If so, I've got two words for you—faint NOT! Don't be discouraged. God is definitely doing a quicker work today concerning the answer to your prayers.

It's not the time to abandon hope or question faith. Lonely times are for getting focused on God and, personally, I've learned to use these wilderness times to become clearer about my calling and my goals. I've found that it's in *these* times that I find out *what* to do, *when* to do it, *where* to do it, and *how* to do it.

Dealing with Hindrances to Answered Prayers

Things are always trying to stop me from getting my prayers answered. They are called hindrances and often, they are spiritual. Knowing that is half the battle. Wilderness times are often testing times, and what they test more than anything are faith and patience.

In 2 Corinthians 4:1, Paul says, *"Therefore seeing we have this ministry, as we have received mercy, we faint not."* The lesson is simple but profound: God has *already* granted mercy (or an answer) to you. All you have to do is not let your faith faint.

**"Faint not" implies the *maintenance*
of strong conviction and strong principle.**

In other words, don't quit! Maintain your stance. Do *not* jump ship! You don't have to pray louder to get God to answer you. He's not hearing impaired. You just have to *faint not*.

Your destiny and destination have *already* been recorded in Heaven. Your answers are *already* coming back to you—fully answered. Think about that for a moment and let it sink in. Realize that your perspective affects everything. So make sure you're thinking faith thoughts. Keep on the high road.

If God has to get an angel to bring back what you're believing for like He did with Daniel, He will do it. Now that ought to make you shout! God is no respecter of persons, but He is a respecter of faith, which is why the Word tells you to faint not.

I believe that success is coming to you spiritually, physically, and financially. Follow my example in this—I don't allow time to defeat my prayers. In those wilderness times (lonely times) I sharpen my goals. Do this. It works!

Don't let any difficulty or danger dishearten you. If you want to be a success going somewhere to succeed, decide that you are going to be one of those "faint not" people. Feelings come and feelings go. Let them! Don't spin in mental circles. Hold fast and feed your faith in God, in yourself, and in your goal.

Inject Yourself with the Word Every Day

The Word never prepares the way for failure or despair—it will build your faith in the worst of times and in the best of times. People of faith don't care what the economic world is doing. We don't stop giving to the Lord or receiving from the Lord. We hold fast. We faint not. We become like God and we change not! This is how we make it through all times, especially tough times.

**Seeking a faith that will keep you from fainting
is a must in tough times. It is supplied
by *constant* hearing of the Word.**

My success over the years hasn't come by accident. I've been injecting myself with the Word every day since 1974. It's like a daily dose of what I need to succeed in what God's called me to do—success for my spirit, soul, and body! The Word is an antidote to failure in life and I believe that you *can* become immune to the whole concept of failure by absorbing the Word and applying it. There is life in the Word that breathes new hope and joy into the heart and mind.

Many people have asked me how it is that I've never had a financial deficit in all my years of ministry. I tell them that I've been immunized with the Word of God.

**When you are immunized with the Word,
you become a good swimmer in the sea of trouble!**

Let the world, people, and even the devil take their best shot. The truth is that greater is He that's in *you* than he that is in the world. You've got what it takes to get through lonely times— wilderness times—you do.

Develop a Stout and Tender Heart

As 2 Corinthians 4:1 says, we have *received* mercy, and so we must also *give* mercy. We must have a stout heart as well as a tender one. A spirit of "faint not" and "give mercy" are a good combination.

Saint Paul refused to faint, even when he was in jail. He gave mercy to the prisoners. In tough times and in good, it is wonderful to show mercy towards others. Show your true colors and give the gift of mercy. Regardless of lonely times or not, you must never change the way you believe God and serve others.

No matter what happens, the only thing that changes in your life is the circumstances. If everything seems to be going the wrong way, pray in the right way.

Your prayers, your mercy towards others, and your giving to the Lord can literally change the course of your life. My wife and I have proven that so many times in our lives and ministry.

When it seemed that nothing was working, we prayed more and we gave more—we used the wilderness time to get clearer on our calling, our goals, and the mission God put on our heart. It confuses people, sure! But it breaks something in the spirit-realm when you lean not to your own understanding, but in all your ways acknowledge God's plan. It breaks something in your own mind to believe the Word instead of the circumstances.

You will develop a stout and tender heart by not giving up, doing the right thing, and using the lonely times to fuel up with the Word and get clearer on your goals. God's people are tough people doing tender things. Whatever circumstance pops up that tries to make you stop praying and stop believing, stop doing or giving don't let it make you do any of that!

Cathy and I learned to use our loneliest times—our wilderness times—to get clearer on our calling and goals. And let me assure you, doing this has worked for us. Year after year, circumstance after circumstance, God never ceases to come through. He is there for us, making a way for us, and helping us to achieve higher levels of success with Him.

This principle will work for you too. Put it to memory and into practice when you find yourself in the wilderness. Not only will you confuse the doubters, but you'll also strengthen yourself far more by having that time than if you didn't.

Absorb the nature of God and fill up with Him when you're in that wilderness place—because if you do, when you leave this time in your life, you're going to walk out stronger and more resilient than when you came. Consider it learning and preparation time. You won't be there forever, so use the time wisely. Regroup. Reestablish. Prepare yourself for the good things in your future.

PRINCIPLE

3

Do Not Seek Approval from People—Listen to God's "Still, Small Voice"

People—if you are trying to succeed God's way, there will always be people in your life who'll try to stop you. Sometimes they don't even realize it and sometimes, they most certainly do, but either way, you will get to a point where you have to ask yourself a question. The question is, "Whose approval am I seeking?"

It is vitally important that you ask yourself this question when the naysayers come because they're coming. You may not think so, but I promise you! No matter how good your idea is, no matter how wonderful your mission, they're coming!

You see, a lot of times God will put something on your heart that other people just don't understand. They don't understand, so they don't approve. They don't approve, so sometimes, they attack. If they did all this silently, it wouldn't be so bad but the worst part is, they tell you! If you point yourself towards success, you will hear things you never thought you'd hear from people you never thought would say such things.

If you're mission is "too much" in any way, expect to hear some junk. Why? A whole lot of people in the world don't like seeing others succeed. So don't be surprised when some people aren't excited about what God put on your heart.

Now the voice of "the naysayer" in your life may be someone you really admire. That happened to me so much in the early years of my ministry, and I have to tell you that, when it happens, it's a real blow. It might come from a person that you highly respect and greatly admire. It might come from someone you love. It may even come from someone you really thought always had your back.

What do you do? Do you follow God? Do you move forward in your goal, your mission, and your heart's desire? Or do you let the voices of people you really respect and even love sway you off-course? That depends on whose approval you are seeking.

Opposing Voices
Get "Delivered from the People"

Sometimes you want to please someone, and you let him or her sway your course. Sometimes the person giving you advice is so respected, you begin to question whether you ever heard the voice of God in your situation. Sometimes you let their naysaying circle around your brain so much that you start to wonder if maybe they are right.

When you are dealing with and weighing opposing voices about your goal, your mission, your dream or the desire of your heart, remember this about voices:

People's voices are always loud and abrupt. God's voice is still, small—and His voice always has a calm and steady strength in it.

In the book of Acts, God used an interesting phrase that relates to not seeking people's approval. He said, *"But rise, and stand upon thy feet: for I have appeared unto thee for this purpose, to make thee a minister and a witness both of these things which thou hast seen, and of those things in the which I will appear unto thee;* **delivering thee from the people**, *and from the Gentiles, unto whom now I send thee"* (Acts 26:16-17).

That is one of the most powerful phrases in the Bible. Use that Word in faith and start saying, "I have been delivered from the people."

In my many years of ministry, I've learned that my job is to please God. It's your job too. **The only One who will *ever* judge you and me in the end is God.**

Is Their Doubt Altering Your Faith?

God always speaks by faith. But sometimes, other people's faith is so low that they can't grasp what God is telling you to do. This happens to me a lot. People will say, "You can't do that!" or "It's impossible!" or "You'll look like a fool if you do that!" I could go on and on.

Now I'm not saying that I won't take advice or counsel. But when that advice goes against the scripture and the voice of God, I don't let it get inside of me. I refuse to let *their* doubt alter *my* faith.

People will doubt you—don't let that change your course. You must understand that they didn't hear what you heard. Your mission and obedience to God should always be first. So, don't get your feelings hurt if your friends are not as committed to what God told you to do.

"Stickability" to My Faith and My Vision

For example, when God told me He wanted us to pay cash for the office buildings of our ministry, some of my best friends said, "You can't do it." You see, they had heard the price of lumber, but I had heard the voice of God for the situation.

Debt seemed like the only way to them, but not me. Why? I knew in my heart that it could be done—and would be done—and my faith in God meant that failure was not an option. Time didn't matter to me. So, I protected my vision in my own mind by not listening to the voices of people who didn't hear what I'd heard from the Lord about the office buildings.

If God has told you to do something, you must protect it at all cost. Don't get rude with anyone. Have mercy. But determine that no matter what anybody says, you will **protect your commitment from the uncommitted.**

People don't like the word "commitment." That word has a lot of hard work, blood, sweat, and tears in it, and there are always people who will discourage you from it.

When we built the ministry buildings, it took every bit of faith and commitment we had. Many people said, "Don't do it that way." Some got angry and quit giving to the ministry when they'd been behind me before. It hurt my feelings because I wanted them to "see it" and believe it with me, but I understood that they just plain couldn't, so I didn't get offended.

Yes, I wanted their approval. I told them what I meant to do. But I can't tell you how many people told me, "Borrow the money, Jesse. Finish it really fast. Just do it." It was tempting. Who doesn't want things fast? But God's still, small voice kept telling me, "You can do it debt-free." So, I decided to stick to God's voice instead of the people's voices.

Well we did it! The ministry buildings are all debt-free today—and we don't have giant amounts of interest to worry about paying back because we wanted everything so quick. We don't have to worry about banks lending us money either. Why? Faith and "stickability." We stood on the Word God had told us instead of going opposite to get people's approval.

In the end, many of those who'd left us naysaying came back and apologized because they saw it work. They could see it and so they understood. But the reason why it worked is because we "saw it" before it ever manifested—that's faith in a nutshell. And it works.

The Earth Remaineth—Harvest Is Coming!

If your seed hasn't come up yet, it will! You know, Cathy and I have never stopped our giving even when we were in the midst of working towards the debt-free buildings.

When family and friends told us we would have to cut back on our giving so that we could do what God told us to do, we said, "NO!" We knew then and we still know now that **our giving produces our future**. We decided that we would live in the blessing.

In Genesis 8:22, it says, *"While the earth remaineth, seedtime and harvest, and cold and heat, and summer and winter, and day and night shall not cease."* Every time I feel the cold or the heat, or see the day or the night, I *know* that my seed will produce a harvest. It doesn't matter what kind of seed it is, it's coming back multiplied. It's just the law of Genesis in effect, and it works with seeds sown to the spirit and seeds sown to the flesh.

Good seeds produce good harvests and bad seeds do the same. Whatever you're sowing, that's what you'll reap—and while many love to focus on this for bad things in life, it's much more important that you focus on the good seeds you're sowing. I believe in giving and I believe in receiving: spiritually, physically, financially, and in every other way. Harvest is coming!

If you think your seed is not working, go outside, tap your foot on the ground, and say really loudly, "The earth remaineth!" Then shout for joy that your harvest is coming. In your mind, your seed and harvest must be seen as just as much of a tangible reality as that ground under your feet that will grow things if you have stickability.

Don't Retreat—It Will Change If You Don't!

I remember a couple who told me that their doctor said they couldn't have children. Do you know what I said? I told them, "Just keep on sowing!" Guess what? They've got a bunch of kids now. In fact, they told me that they don't want any more!

The Word works. God told those people, and I did too, to *"Be fruitful, and multiply"* (Genesis 1:22). The doctor went by what *he saw*. That's the natural way. The faith way is always to go by what *you say*—and if you don't know what to say, then open your Bible! Say what it says. That's what that couple did and between their faith in the Word and their sowing, they produced a harvest of kids!

Never retreat from a difficult situation. The situation will change if you don't. It doesn't take much work to become a loser in life and to me, the greatest losers are the ones who refuse to believe in the potential God gave them and just give up because they don't want to see ahead to what could be.

I'd rather be a lonely winner in life than to be stuck in a room with a bunch of losers who have no visionary sight for what "can be" and are content to live in a state of mediocrity while talking about everything bad in life. I don't like when people cut down others for dreaming, doing, and just plain wanting a good life. Success is wonderful, and I believe that God can help any of us to create it.

Nobody and no situation is hopeless, and I believe everyone has the potential to be an everyday visionary—to use faith in God and His Word to create a good future and have success in life.

Not long ago, I was with a bunch of ministers that were talking about how bad everything was. I knew it was time to change that environment. I said, "Gentlemen, everything you are talking about is what you *see*"—they knew I was talking about their natural eyes and what they perceive situations to be. Then I said, "I never tell God what I have; I tell Him what I *want*." They looked at me with astonishment.

Then I said, "What do you *want?*" The room started to change. I said, "*Say* that, *believe* that, and you'll *have* that." It switched the conversation in a moment. We moved from doubt to faith in an instant, and faith is what works.

So, what do *you* want? Whatever is burning in your heart and you want to happen—*say* that and you shall *have* that. Don't fall into the trap of just going by your natural eyes. Look up to

God and look ahead. Determine that you are in the business of speaking by faith and seeking the approval of God—not people.

PRINCIPLE
4

Is There Not a Cause? Passion is the Power that Creates Life and Helps You Achieve Success

God is no respecter of persons If He will bless me, He will bless you. But He is most certainly a respecter of faith. If there's one thing I've done all my life, it's never get lax about what I've wanted. I learned from a very, very young age that passion for anything is vital to success.

I think King David is a good example of how being passionate about your cause can change the course of your life. David asked a simple question to those who were around him in 1 Samuel 17:29. He was young and had gone out to bring food to his brothers when they were dealing with Goliath and the Philistine army.

They didn't approve of him being there and taunted him that he just came to see the battle. I love David's response because it was simple and true. He said, "Is there not a cause?"

Even though David was just a teenager, he understood what to do in a difficult situation. He knew Goliath had defied the nation of Israel. In his mind, King Saul and the army of Israel had **lost their passion and forgotten their cause**.

Many people today who do not achieve their goals have that same problem. If you want success in life, you must *stay passionate* and *remember the cause*. It's called "stay the course!" Protect this principle at all costs.

What made David a great king was his passion to believe God. And from that passion, he became a doer, and that prepared a pathway for his future life as king. He slew that giant with faith and one small stone...and everyone saw it.

Don't Give All Your Attention to Your Enemy

What was happening before David showed up? Israel was listening to what Goliath was saying instead of what God was saying—they were giving all their attention to what their enemy was saying and doing. It kept them mentally and emotionally defeated.

To be a success, you must determine that you won't give all of your time and attention to the obstacles defying your future success. Give all your time and attention to what *God* has placed in your heart—guard your heart.

If God has given you a desire, then you must achieve it.

Whatever God has put on your heart, you need to be passionate about it. Remember that God gave you that desire so that you could complete your destiny and reach your destination—if it's in your heart, it's there for a reason.

If you don't know what sparks your passion, pray and ask Him to reveal what is in your heart. Don't pay attention at the beginning to any "thing" or "person" beyond God—because there is a reason why you are passionate about one thing and not another. Boil that passion down to its root in your mind—what do you really want? Why do you want it? What's the reason? You'll find out what you really want when you find out where your passion lays—and the tip is to never make an excuse for the blessings of God or the visions, goals, and plans for success He's put in your heart.

I'm Passionate About My Ministry

I constantly say to myself, "Is there not a cause?" I do it even when my body is tired or finances are threatening to dry up. Why? Because God saved me from a hellish life when I was 24 years old—and I know what it is like to live without God, even if you are financially successful doing it.

I know what's it's like to be rich and I know what it's like to be poor—and while rich is better, both are equally miserable places without God. I thought "success" was just money. I was so disappointed when I realized money couldn't make me happy. It just made me more comfortable in my misery.

I'm passionate about my ministry because I'm passionate about seeing people saved, lifted up, and at peace with God and themselves—so that they can go and do what God made them to do in the first place!

Thinking about the state of the world, the state of humanity, and knowing that God can change everything for others like He changed everything for me so long ago is one way I keep my passion alive.

I don't sit around being depressed by the state of the world. I don't deny it's bad. I choose instead to refuse to be distracted from the cause. I keep my cause at the forefront of my mind because I know what could be and can be if only people would receive the Lord and begin to retrain their minds with His Word, so that they produce the fruit of His Spirit.

The fruit of His Spirit is Galatians 5:22-23—love, joy, peace, longsuffering, gentleness, goodness, faith, meekness, and self-control. If every person in the world had that producing and flowing in their life, nobody would break the law or harm anyone intentionally—they'd be too focused on living a good life and making life better for those around them.

It's my joy and my job to take as many to Heaven with me as I can, and to help as many as I can to be successful, from the spirit first all the way to whatever dreams God has put on their hearts to pursue. I believe in success, God's way! Because without Him, anything masquerading as success is fleeting, temporary, and amounts to zero in the end.

The reason I started this ministry is because of the cause of Christ. My vision is the Great Commission that Jesus gave to His disciples: *"Go ye into all the world, and preach the Gospel to every creature"* (Mark 16:15). Saving and salvaging people by bringing the redemption and restoration of Christ into their lives is the cause—and it's too great a cause to give up.

Don't let Today's Little Things Steal Your Future Big Thing

It's very natural to look at the natural circumstances standing in your way when you have a big cause and big goals to help you fulfill that cause. Your mind often wants to get you into a state of worry over all the logistics it will take to do what you've got in your heart to do, all the situations or even people in your way.

I like to call these little things. Sure they seem big but in reality, they are just like Goliath in the end—one stone's-throw away from being insignificant!

It's tempting to fixate on whatever it is that you lack—but if David did that, he would never have stepped out onto battle. He never would have picked up one stone. If he had focused on Goliath's size instead of the size of his God, he would never have had the passion to do the unthinkable and go head to head with a very big boy!

In other words, if David hadn't focused on God, he would not only have missed his opportunity to help the army of Israel that day, but he also would have forfeited his future as king of Israel.

Don't let the little things that are trying to mock you and torment your mind steal the big thing that is in your future. What are the little things? Not long ago, I was reading Matthew 6:31, *"Therefore take no thought, saying, What shall we eat? or, What shall we drink? or, Wherewithal shall we be clothed?"*

You can't live without food. You can't live without water. And nobody wants to see you walking around naked! Those things are important! But Jesus taught that He didn't want us dwelling over and over on these kinds of things—it showed us that God's best for our life isn't to live in a state of worry.

What you think, you will become—so don't waste precious real estate in your mind by letting worry-filled thoughts run your life. They'll steal your destiny, if you do because they'll creep out of your mind and start dripping out of your mouth. That's called worry-filled speech and it's a seemingly small little thing that in actuality will steal your big future.

Your future is in your mouth—so say what you want and not what you have. Look at your God and have faith. David changed the course of his life with passion. It's the power that created a new life for him and helped him achieve the cause.

Don't *say* what you *think*, just say what God says!

Reel your thoughts in and put your trust in Him because the reality is that you are serving a God whose streets are gold! He created this earth and He can take care of earthly stuff!

Notice that Jesus was so passionate about what He believed that He could easily say, "Don't even think about those things!" Wow, that's big! You see, Jesus knew what His Father would do. He said it in the next verse, *"For your heavenly Father knoweth that ye have need of all these things"* (Matthew 6:32).

God *knows* what you need. He knows what you want. Worrying about these things doesn't help anything. Jesus told us what to do, *"But seek ye first the kingdom of God, and His righteousness; and all these things shall be added unto you"* (Matthew 6:33). In other words, put your passion and attention where it belongs.

You see, you're going to get "all these things" you want and need when you put your passion towards what God wants and needs—His cause and His way of doing things. Passion for Him will lead you to greater levels of trust, and then blessings come! So, don't let your natural mind rule your mouth. Refuse to stand in the way of your own blessing.

Rid Yourself of Uninvited Thoughts

Apply this principle to your life. When thoughts of lack, sickness, or worry come into your mind say, "Those are not my thoughts! I don't and I won't dwell on those things!" You see, your mind is not a depository for everything negative that has no faith in God. You have been given the mind of Christ! Thoughts may come in uninvited, but they're not *your* thoughts. So don't take them and don't let them roll around in your head—because, remember, that you *take* them when you *say* them!

I want you to achieve total success in every spiritual and tangible way in life. I hope you take ownership of the Word of God, the cause of Christ, and the desire that God has put in your life. Your heart's desires are your cause. Stay passionate about them and keep moving forward.

Passion is powerful. I pray you will refuse to waste your passion on things you don't want and I hope you instead, focus with passion on what God has put in your heart and wants for your life.

Remember, passion is the power that creates life and helps you achieve your cause! So, is there a cause? Yes! Do it!

PRINCIPLE
5

Don't Settle for the Land of Better—
Aim to Dwell in the Land of Best

You Will Empower Others
Through Your Example

God didn't create you to just barely get by. I believe He created you to achieve total success in this life—spiritually, physically, and even financially if you want that. In any area you want to succeed, the desire to reach your goal is necessary.

This is why one of the ways you can hinder your future success is to become overly satisfied when things get a little better. When things move from bad to a little better you must resist the urge to stop believing that God can do even more for you.

Years of bad teaching has many believers thinking that success in and of itself is bad—that it's greedy to believe for something better, and that's simply not true. God loves you and wants you to have the best. You just have to want the same for yourself to move beyond a little better.

Avoid Complacency at All Costs

Let me give you an example. When God took the children of Israel out of the land of Egypt, He didn't mean for them to spend their entire lives in the wilderness. Of course, they were excited to leave the land of not enough (Egypt) and they easily became satisfied to get by with a little better in the wilderness the land of just enough.

Beware of becoming complacent. For the children of Israel, the wilderness was better than Egypt, but God didn't want them to spend their lives in better. God wanted them to move on to what was best. Best wasn't the desert wilderness, even though they were free from slavery. Best was a life lived in the Promised Land, a land not just of freedom, but of abundance—a land that flowed with milk and honey.

I heard someone say that they came out of the land of not enough, and went to the land of just enough, but God wanted them to live in the land of more than enough. That about sums it up!

In Joshua 1:2-3, God says:

Moses My servant is dead; now therefore arise, go over this Jordan, thou, and all this people, unto the land which I do give to them, even to the children of Israel.

Every place that the sole of your foot shall tread upon, that have I given unto you, as I said unto Moses.

God was telling Joshua to get up—to arise—because the people had gotten satisfied with just surviving. This is a dangerous mindset to be in. I believe that this mindset stops people more than anything else from reaching the goals God put on their heart.

Complacency in any area (spiritual, physical, financial, or otherwise) will keep you bound in the land of just enough. God means for all of us to follow Him and to rule and reign as His kings and His priests in this life it means we have to realize that we are "just passing through."

Refuse to Live in the Valley
It Is Only a Path to Your Promise

I refuse to live in a place that God wants me to pass through. The wilderness was a path for the children of Israel. It was never supposed to be their destiny. It was a passageway and nothing more. In Psalms, it says:

*Yea, though I walk **through** the valley of the shadow of death, I will fear no evil: for Thou art with me; Thy rod and Thy staff they comfort me.*

Thou preparest a table before me in the presence of mine enemies: Thou anointest my head with oil; my cup runneth over.

Surely goodness and mercy shall follow me all the days of my life: and I will dwell in the house of the LORD forever.

Psalm 23:4-6

This is talking about abundance with God, and it begins by telling us to walk "through" the valley. Notice that it didn't say to stop, build a house, and live in the valley!

You'd be surprised how many people think that death valley (I call it "survival valley") is where God wants them to live. You have to shake off this way of thinking! It's important that you begin to think like God thinks, and you do that by renewing your mind. God told Joshua:

> *This book of the law **shall not depart out of thy mouth**; but thou shalt **meditate** therein day and night, that thou mayest observe to **do according to all** that is written therein: for **then thou shalt make thy way prosperous**, and **then thou shalt have good success**. Have not I commanded thee? **Be strong** and of a **good courage**; be not afraid, neither be thou dismayed: for **the LORD thy God is with thee** whithersoever thou goest.*

> Joshua 1:8-9

I know that's a long passage of scripture, but it is your vehicle to achieving success in whatever you are believing God for and setting your mind to do. Complacency is a cancer that can stop you from fulfilling your destiny and reaching your destination in life. Decide today that you are never going to live anywhere else but the land of more than enough.

I believe that you and I must be examples to others not only through our words, but also through our lifestyle. I said it earlier; it empowers others when we lead by example.

Life is a Journey
Take as Many People with You as You Can

Success attracts attention. We must be giving God glory— spiritually, physically, and financially. Never make an excuse for living the blessed life. Just tell people that you're giving God glory in everything you do. Life is a journey and you might as well take as many people with you as you can as you make your way—there is so much joy in including others.

When you refuse to be complacent and aim for your goals and dreams, you will empower others through your example. Without even saying anything, they'll watch you and you'll inspire them. So, it's vital to all of us that you aim for your own personal "land of best!"

Sometimes, to break the comfort-zone mentality that makes you want to get lax, you just have to say it aloud to yourself, "I will live in the land of more than enough. The land of best is where God wants me to be and I'm going!"

Lighting a fire under yourself works. Speaking the end-result works. A lot of people don't believe it, but it doesn't matter—it's still true. I pray and I say what I want every day. I suggest you do the same, and keep doing it, until you arrive where you want to be—spiritually, physically, financially, or in any other area you want to focus on in life.

Speak favor over your life—say things like, "I have favor with both God and man. God is making a way for me." Speak blessings over your life—"I will harvest on every seed I sow! I will be blessed in the city, blessed in the field, blessed coming in and blessed going out!"

If at all possible, find someone who will pray in agreement with you for what you want. There is power in agreement. Jesus said, "*... That if two of you shall agree on earth as touching any thing that they shall ask, it shall be done for them of My Father which is in Heaven*" (Matthew 18:19).

Things will get in your way—this is just a part of going anywhere in life. There are hurdles to cross and things to overcome. That's part of the journey and what makes the success that much more sweet.

I like to think of whatever stands in my way like the Jordan River of the Bible. It's an obstacle in my path, yes, but it's something I'm crossing over. Whatever your spiritual, physical, or financial Jordan River is, just remember that it's not going to be in your way forever because you are crossing over it.

God will make the way if you focus on Him and where you want to be. So set your eyes on the other side. Look more at the land than the water in front of you, because it's time for the blessing to flow to you.

If the people you share your heart with ask you, "Do you believe this stuff?" tell them, "No, I *live* this stuff!" That will get their attention. Help them to see how much potential there is in always having faith in God. Remember, life is a journey anyway. You may as well set your eyes and your faith in the direction of total success.

Never let anybody tell you that you can't live in the land of *best*. After all, you are God's child and that alone gives you the right to live blessed—on earth, like you would be living in Heaven, just like the "Our Father" prayers says:

Thy will be done in earth, as it is in Heaven.

Matthew 6:10

I encourage you to be bold enough to not only pray this, but endeavor to live this! The will of God for you is totally encapsulated in the place named Heaven that He created—and if that's not the land of best I don't know what is!

Think of Heaven for a minute and allow yourself to feel what you imagine you'll feel there—that's pure success you're feeling. It's peace. Joy. No sickness. People in harmony and prosperity everywhere you look. Yes, prosperity. It's not a dirty word. If gold streets weren't important to God, He wouldn't have put them there or mentioned it. He wants you to think higher. It's concrete to Him, so I don't believe for a minute that He has a problem with you having some financial success in life, if you want it!

My prayer for you is that God's will be done right here on earth as it is in Heaven—in your life! I pray that you'll refuse complacency. I pray you'll create the life you want with your mind, your mouth, and the wonderful Word of God!

PRINCIPLE
6

Don't Judge Others—It Opens Up Your Life to Major Leaks

Judging others is a waste of spiritual energy. The best way to fail is to fall into the trap of judging others. When you let yourself focus on the negative things someone has going on or has said about you, you're doing only one thing—getting distracted! It'll pull you right off course every time. You can't focus on what you need to do when you're focusing on judging somebody else! I've said it before and I'll say it again: never let a *distraction* become an *attraction*.

You Can Cause Major Energy Leaks In Your Own Life

To achieve success in life, your energy must not stagnate in the area of distractions. It must go in the right direction—God's direction, the good direction—and the place He has intended you to go.

**Don't judge others because you will open yourself up to major "leaks" in your life.
Let God, Who is the Higher Power, handle that.**

In Matthew 7:1-2, Jesus said, *"Judge not, that ye be not judged. For with what judgment ye judge, ye shall be judged: and with what measure ye mete, it shall be measured to you again."*

If there is one thing I've learned in life, it's this: obey what God says! One of the greatest statements I've ever heard came from the mouth of Billy Graham, and it was on this exact subject. Dr. Graham said, "It is the Father's job to judge. It is the Holy Spirit's job to convict. And it is *our* job to love." Now that's powerful. That's wisdom!

We should never try to do God's job. Neither should we try to do the Holy Spirit's job. We have **the job of a lifetime** and that job is **to *love***.

If you start judging others, you can take it to the bank that "cracks" in your life will manifest. God's work in your life will slow to a crawl. Your prayers will go unanswered. Your peace will slowly be eroded while your irritation with life in general will go up.

You Can Open a Door You Don't Really Want to Open

Not only does judging ruin our focus and sidetrack our progress towards our own personal success, but I believe it opens a spiritual door for the devil to come in swiftly and bring problems and pain that we don't need in life.

When we, as believers, waste our time judging one another and feeding into the mindset of strife, I believe that we even can hinder spiritual movements that we really need. We cancel out unity when we choose to judge.

Some of the greatest revivals in history were stopped because people started judging other people. What once was wonderful turned into something different. The Spirit stopped flowing, money dried up, and God's work was stopped in its tracks. I've seen people lose everything they've had and completely walk away from God, when all they really had to do was shut their mouths and focus on loving.

How many times does the Word remind us to love? Scriptures like, *"Bless them that curse you"* and *"Pray for them which despitefully use you"* are reminders to us to love instead of judge.

I know it is not easy, but if God said we should do it, then we *can* do it. He would not tell us to do something that we were incapable of doing. We can stop judging and start *loving*.

Yes, Speak the Truth—But Speak It in Love

Speaking the truth in love about something is not judging. The Bible instructs us to speak the truth and tells us that the truth will set us free. So speaking the truth is not being critical, it's simply being truthful! But the motive must be in love, not in judgment.

I once heard someone say that if you speak the truth, you can walk away and forget everything you've said because the truth can stand alone through anything. It is simple and pure.

Jesus said, *"I am the Way, the Truth, and the Life: no man cometh unto the Father, but by Me"* (John 14:6). If you really want to be a success in life, don't focus on what they say. Focus on what God says.

Sometimes the Leak Is Just Too Expensive

Many times I've been asked about how other ministries do their business. People want me to gossip and pass judgment, to let them in on what they think I may know about this ministry or that ministry. I've often said, "I don't know about their business, I'm about my Father's business." I learned that from Jesus!

You see, the goal that God has given me is too big for me to waste my time and effort on putting my nose into someone else's business! I don't want to put my focus in the wrong place. I consider that a "leak" that is just too expensive.

My goal is to reach people and change lives, one soul at a time—that is the destiny and destination of this ministry. It was Jesus' goal and it's mine too. I believe that God notices everything. A recording is being done with every action and motive, and I believe that God gets excited when we choose to love instead of judge.

I'll be honest with you. It hurts me when people say nasty things about me. I'm so tempted to not only judge them, but also hurt them! I'll admit it. I'm still human! But I've decided that no matter how I initially feel, I've got to let mercy and forgiveness flow because my mission in life is too important to forfeit to judgment.

The net of love that needs to be cast is too important to allow judgment to tear it apart. The world and the people in it are too important to allow any more room for the devil and all his works.

So when I'm hurt, when I'm angry, or when I just plain feel tempted to do it, I do my best to rise above judging others. I just go beyond it. I remind myself that the cause of Christ is too great, the leaks are too expensive, and there's nothing worth hindering the move of God on this earth.

We are the body of Christ. We've got better things to do! Personally and as a group, it's time to stop wasting time and springing energy-leaks by judging one another. Let's focus on doing good to one another, and especially if we are of the household of faith!

PRINCIPLE

7

Listening Will Help You to See Your Situation in New Ways

This is one of the most important things I do to achieve success. Let me explain. When you learn to listen instead of always talk, you will find that you gain new concepts, insights, and ideas. Listening is about being still and absorbing what is around you. It's a state of receiving. It's about listening to other people, of course, but it's also and most importantly about listening to God.

Faith for Your Mission Can't Rise Until You Listen

In Proverbs 4:20 it says, *"My son, attend to My words; incline thine ear unto My sayings."* Notice that it is *hearing* God's words that brings faith (Romans 10:17).

When you listen to His words, revelations will come—and those revelations can change your life forever. God has exactly what you need spiritually, physically, financially, and in every other facet of your life. But the faith and inspiration you need to actually do what you want to do can't rise up until you learn to *listen.*

You *will* find success in anything you do if you listen to God's words and follow the revelations He gives you. If you are willing to simply *listen*, I can tell you that faith *will* rise up in your heart. It will give you the inspiration to get up and move on your goals.

Faith can rise up not only by hearing God's word, but also by hearing other people's words. God will use others to stir you into action—which is why listening to others is so important too.

Don't Just Ponder—*Produce!*

When it comes to revelations from God, people seem to like to think and talk about them. But God doesn't want you to just *ponder*—He wants you to *produce!* He doesn't give you a revelation just to tickle your ears and make you feel spiritual. He gives you insight so that you can create *change* in your life and in the world around you.

You do not serve a passive God. He's active and He created you to create—to move, to change, to learn, to flourish, and to grow *all* the days of your life. I often say that dreams have no expiration date. Growing is not just for the young!

It does not matter how old or how young you are, you can do something for God and for others. You can produce! There's energy in *doing,* and producing will add more joy to your life than pondering ever will!

I find that the Church talks a lot about healing, prosperity, love, and faith, but how many of those things do you actually see produced? **Success is abundant and it's *everywhere*.** Listen and look for it. Do it, even if everybody around you is stuck in the negative-minded mud.

Somebody's got to have light! You have it inside of you. Use it! Anybody can point out what's going down the drain. Anybody can worry and hunker down in fear. The more you focus your attention on what's bad, the harder it will be for you to listen for God's good revelation—and I promise you that His words and ways are what will motivate you to rise up and produce.

Seeing Things in a Different Way

Inspiration from God can come in many different ways and from all sorts of people. You must not only *hear* the Word itself that is spoken, but also *how* someone says it—because listening like that can change *everything*.

Listening will inspire you. God will use a method or a person you never thought He would use to get you to see a different way to do something. Success is *always* on God's mind for you.

In 2 Peter 3:15-18, Peter is talking about the many revelations of the apostle Paul. At that time, and even today, many people consider Paul's gospel hard to be understood—even Peter himself thought that. Yet, Paul's gospel is the whole foundation of what it means to be in Christ. By the time it was all said and done, the man wrote two-thirds of the New Testament! Yet, they called him *"hard."*

Thank God that Peter had the foresight to *listen* to Paul and encourage all of us to do the same. Paul was the one who told us that we could go boldly to the throne of grace and obtain what we need from the Lord (Hebrews 4:16)—and that is what I call success in ALL things!

Sure, some of Paul's sayings are hard. But for those of us willing to listen anyway, Paul's revelations have literally changed our lives—spiritually, physically, and even financially. Read it for yourself! The apostle Paul will cause you to see things in a completely different way!

I like to call the apostle Paul "The ALL Preacher." He had an understanding of God's nature as a provider. In Philippians 4:19 he says, *"But my God shall supply all your need according to His riches in glory by Christ Jesus."* The emphasis is on the word *all*—not just some of your needs, but *all* of them. Go ahead and shout!

One Woman's Life-Changing Words

Years ago, Cathy and I went to visit a friend's ministry to see how they did things. A lady there told us we needed to get an aircraft for our ministry travels. She had looked at our packed preaching schedule in our monthly magazine and knew that this tool would be a vital part in fulfilling our vision for world evangelism. I told her that Cathy and I were believing God for our own aircraft, but first, we were focused on our plan to purchase more television time for our weekly broadcast.

She looked at us and simply said, "Why don't you do both at the same time?" Now, the *way* she said that statement stirred something up in my wife, Cathy, and I. Sure, we knew that God *could* do that, but no one had ever said it as *easily* as that. It was such a simple thing to say, but profound—and Cathy and I were inspired.

That woman caused us to look at our situation in a new way. Cathy and I hadn't realized we were really limiting God and ourselves. But, immediately, that woman's words inspired us. We could have shrugged her comment off like it was nothing and stayed thinking the same way as before. No. We chose to listen.

We left that day and declared to ourselves that we would do it all at the same time. Listening had stirred our faith. And do you know what? Getting our first aircraft and increasing airtime at the same time was the easiest thing we had ever believed God for. The truth is that the lady believed in us more than we believed in ourselves!

From that day on, our whole way of doing things at our ministry changed. Now, when God gives us a project, we don't limit our mind the way we once did. We have no problem having multiple projects going on, because we know God can handle it!

Now, what the woman said to us wasn't exactly the word of God—scripture and verse—but it was filled with faith that can only come from the word! God used her to change us. Thank God we listened!

Listening to that woman's simple statement made Cathy and I realize that we had limited God's vision for us in the past. But today, things are different! Today, we don't just walk by faith, we run by faith! We run the course that has been set before us knowing that we will finish it.

We aren't afraid to do big things for God. We know He is limitless, and so we've chosen to take the limits off. Why not? It's all faith anyway!

Work on the art of listening. Listen to God—it will surge your faith. Listen to people—you'll know instinctively when they say something that inspires you. (You'll also know when to just let their words roll off your back and into the trashcan!)

The more you listen, the more you'll see things differently and be inspired to run the race set before you with power and grace—listening is one of the greatest principles for success you will ever apply. Do more of it and see for yourself.

PRINCIPLE
8

Respect the Royalty in Yourself and Others

We are all important. In Revelation 1:6 it says, "*And hath made us kings and priests unto God and His Father; to Him be glory and dominion for ever and ever. Amen.*"

That verse tells you *who* you are—it defines your future. As believers, we *must* give God glory. We *must* honor His right to dominion forever and ever. That's a big statement!

How do we do it? Well, one of the ways we can keep bringing glory to God and establishing His dominion is to step into our rightful roles of authority.

As believers, we have been *made* by God to be **kings** and **priests** for Him. That's why we must have respect for each other. That's why we must honor one another, if nothing more than for our authority under God.

When we don't respect and honor one another, God can't be glorified. We actually dishonor *His* authority when we dismiss our *own*.

Dominion for the Sake of Respect

Notice the Lord didn't make us paupers and beggars—He made us kings and priests. Some of us are more kingly, some more priestly, and some of us are a combination of both. But no matter where we are strongest, we must recognize our corporate *dominion*.

Kings and priests have dominion and that means authority over a domain. We *rule* over things. We *control* things. We *own* things. **Dominion** is what we're called to *do*.

We are part of a kingdom and that kingdom is the Kingdom of God. It is an organized, united, and whole kingdom founded and run by the Lord. And it should be consolidated with unity in order to run harmoniously. That's why we should always respect each other. Making that effort helps to keep the wheels moving smoothly.

In fact, for the sake of respect, we should make a concentrated effort *not* to cut one another down, but to stand up for each other when under fire. When people start saying bad things around me about someone I know, I usually try to stop them by saying something like, "Excuse me, you must have them on your mind. So let's pray for them right now." Most people are shocked when I do that. They just expect me to get into judgment mode, especially if the person they're talking about actually deserves it!

You see, I don't want to stop God's plan for my life. I don't want to stop His anointing on my ministry or my future prosperity. I refuse to open a door to strife in my life. You see, that person they may want to cut down is a king and a priest.

Now, they may be a *bad* king or priest, but that's between them and God! For me to get into strife over it is wrong. Again,

God didn't make you or me the judge and jury over someone else's life.

The Altar of Opportunity

Our focus should be on living "in Christ." The person who lives *in* Christ and *for* Christ lives by principles—and not just any principles, but by the truth found in the Word of God. The Word should shape your principles.

Your inner principles will rule your thoughts and shape your opinions, ideas, doctrines, and creeds. They will actually propel you in a certain direction in life day by day. That's why number eight in this list is so important—Respect the royalty in each other. When you recognize the royalty in others, it helps you to treat them with more honor.

God is the One Who gives us the means of rendering service and blessing to others. I like to call this "the altar of opportunity." In other words, when I have the opportunity to bless, I should do it as unto the Lord—because I'm literally bringing Him glory by blessing others with that kind of respect.

If someone doesn't deserve respect, that's still okay. My altar of opportunity will become an altar of sacrifice. Sometimes it doesn't feel good. But I am not moved by feelings; I am moved by faith. Glory!

Ruling the Kingdom Within Yourself

The Kingdom of God, which is the Church, should have respect and love for the Lord and for one another. You and I are the heirs of the kingdom's privileges. We are the ones who make it function properly. Our purpose? *"To Him be glory and dominion for ever and ever!"*(Revelation 1:6) We can never lose sight of our purpose as kings and priests.

I believe the man who does the will of God rules his kingdom within himself. Self-rule is one of the first lessons that Jesus Christ taught His disciples. If you can't rule yourself, then you can't rule anything!

Jesus warned us in Luke 6:42 not to bother picking out specks in other people's eyes until we've first removed the planks of wood from our own. We must rule ourselves first.

Waste Not, Want Not
It's a Matter of Respect

The truth is that everything God has given you must be ruled over with respect. For example, if you don't respect money, it will ruin you. I'm serious! Money must be respected.

One of the best sermons I believe the Lord ever gave me was *"Fragments—Waste Not and You'll Want Not: Your Riches are in Your Fragments."* That sermon is so important because it deals with respecting and valuing the things that are in your hands—realizing that there are riches in the little things if we would only take the time to gather them up.

The story of the fishes and loaves in John chapter six shows the importance of respect and sustenance. Jesus respected that little boy's fish dinner. He refused for people to waste any of it.

That's why Jesus commanded His disciples to pick up the leftovers after the multitude had eaten: *"When they were filled, He said unto His disciples, Gather up the fragments that remain, that nothing be lost"* (John 6:12).

Respect made Jesus do that. *Honor* made Jesus do that. He counted not only the seed as precious, but he respected the boy who sowed the seed. Jesus did not discount him because he was a child. He honored the boy. He didn't throw away the fragments of the miracle. He made sure every last bit was picked up.

The lesson is that there is value in the people around you and value in the small things—because they aren't small. What often looks like little bits when scattered is usually a lot more than you think. The disciples gathered twelve baskets full of bread and fish that day—and that is a lot!

Success is hard to maintain when you're unaware of the fragments in your life. Wasting is a sure-shot to losing. Respecting what comes to you, along with the people in your path is crucial to being a godly success.

So I encourage you to take this principle to heart and begin to recognize the kingship and priesthood in your fellow believers—and don't be wasteful. Start to work on seeing everyone in the Body of Christ like family. Some may be closer family and others may be extended family, but they are all connected to you in a very important way.

Honor others. It's the right thing to do Because when you respect others, it shows that you respect yourself. It's one way you honor the Lord. Never forget it: You have a rightful and wonderful position in Christ, and so do others. We are all kings and priests under our Lord Jesus. So don't hold back. Respect the royalty that is all around you.

PRINCIPLE
9

Always Keep Encouragement
Close to Your Heart

It's the Oxygen of the Soul

I hope you're enjoying these principles. They really have helped me in my own life and it's my prayer that they help you too. Now, onto the next one! This particular life principle has brought great comfort to me. It's short but sweet—and works when you feel like life is just hitting you from all sides. This one is about finding your strength.

Encouragement is the Oxygen of the Soul

Everybody needs to be encouraged sometimes. We all get weary from time to time—and what helps you to "faint not" and keep on going can sometimes be simple encouragement.

Encouragement will help you to breathe in difficult times. It is like oxygen for a weary soul. Seeking it out and keeping it close to your heart is critical to achieving godly success. So, don't fool yourself into thinking it's unimportant or something that doesn't really matter. Encouragement matters! It gives your soul the restful boost you need to move forward.

I'm known all over the world as an encourager. It's such an honor when people say that to me. It brings tears to my eyes and warmness to my heart. I had a hard life as child and had very little encouragement. Honestly, I learned to encourage people from examples in the Bible. It's also how I learned to encourage myself.

In 1 Samuel 30:6 it says, *"But David encouraged himself in the Lord his God."* Notice how personal David was with God Almighty. The word *encouraged* also means *strength*.

Today I find so many people under such stress. In the middle of it all, many forget how close God really is—they lose sight of the personal nature of our God. All we have to do is call upon God and He will answer. I mean that's it!

God is always near and always ready to answer. He is our senior partner in this life, but we have to rely on Him and find our strength in Him. It's got to be personal. That's why David could write in Psalm 23:1, *"The Lord is my Shepherd; I shall not want."* Those few little words contain a massive amount of encouraging revelation on what it is like to really trust, adhere, and rely on the Lord—it actually pushes you past "wanting."

A Pathway of Hope

You have to encourage yourself first before you can encourage others. I call that self-preservation! You can't *give* strength to others unless you *have* strength within yourself.

Some of the best conversations I've ever had have been with myself! How can I say that? Because the Bible says, *"Faith comes by hearing and hearing by the Word of God"* (Romans 10:17) and, years ago, I decided to start speaking the Word not just over myself, but also to myself as a way to gain encouragement.

I began breathing in my own encouragement—and it was like oxygen from God Himself, lifting my soul and infusing me with faith. I still do this today. In fact, I do it every day. Why? Because I know that encouragement works—and the Word produces faith. And faith is vital to godly success.

Your faith in God is what gives shape and force to your actions. Your faith is what opens up a pathway of hope for you.

Hebrews 11:1 says, *"Now faith is the substance of things hoped for, the evidence of things not seen."* That verse is a Christian truth—and Christian truth will always bring Christian provision.

If you are feeling heavily pressured about something, your faith will revive as you grasp that promise in Hebrews 11:1. Do not forget where the strength of your faith is. Again, it's Hebrew 11:1! Here's a good example of this.

Daniel's Unflinching Faith

One of the greatest statesmen God ever created was the prophet Daniel. His life was filled with ups and downs, but he did not flinch. He knew where his strength was—it was in his faith in God and his faith in himself.

Daniel *always* consulted with God. His relationship and fellowship with God produced great faith. Daniel's faith in God was his strong foundation—and it was so strong that he didn't even fight the lions in the den. Were those lions hungry? Was Daniel their meat? Yes and yes!

Most people would have lost their minds in fear. But not Daniel. Instead of screaming or fidgeting or fighting, Daniel looked around at his situation and knew that there was nothing left that he could do except have faith. So, he didn't fret, worry, or flinch. He simply sat down amongst the lions and waited for his rescue.

Daniel had faith in God. His faith created a calm in his emotions, and that calm radiated in the lions' den, right in the midst of a life or death situation. Even the hungry lions noticed that calm—and the Lord shut their mouths.

See Your *Coming* Victories

God always knows where we are. There is no point to rage with fear when encouraging yourself in God brings so much calm. As I've said so many times, tough times don't last but tough people do. I expect results from my faith *all* the time. I never look at where I *am*. I always look at where I want to *go*.

If I'm in the valley, I start looking up at the mountains. Are you getting this? Start painting pictures in your mind of *coming* victories. Remember that you can't encourage anyone else until you encourage yourself—so do it!

I don't know about you, but I just don't have time to wait around for someone else to encourage me all the time. I encourage myself! And it sure feels good to breathe a big gulp of that!

There are scriptures for every problem that will lift you up so that you can breathe easy. Seek them out. Read them. Study them. Then, encourage yourself with them. I love 2 Corinthians 9:8, *"And God is able to make all grace abound toward you; that ye, always having all sufficiency in all things, may abound to every good work."*

That verse works in so many areas for me and reminds me that I will always have everything I need to do the work God has called me to do. I love to breathe in that scripture and exhale encouragement. Then, I go about my way refreshed and able to give to others too. Are you getting the picture?

Don't underestimate the power of encouragement. It brings calm to hairy situations and paves the way for success. Plus, it just plain feels good! So keep encouragement close to your heart—see it as the oxygen of the soul, and a very important key to your success.

*

PRINCIPLE
10

Always Be Generous—Take as Many To the Top with You as You Can

Have you ever heard someone say, "It's lonely at the top"? I'm sure you have. Lots of people work hard to achieve success only to turn around one day and realize that they're all alone with their blessings. Why? Because those kinds of people made it to the top only thinking of themselves, but true success is never a solitary adventure.

This principle will help you to not only achieve success in your own life, but to do it without alienating people in the process. It's number ten on my list and it is this: Always be generous—take as many with you to the top as you can.

Let the Generosity of Christ Flow Through You

Jesus isn't a religious figure to me. He's the *living* God to me, living in me, and helping me to live the life He's given me and fulfill the calling on my life to help others find Him. The Spirit of the Lord is generous! And I believe that His generous Spirit should be at the heart of everything we believers do.

Letting the generosity of Christ flow through you means opening up your life and your blessings to others because that is essentially what Jesus did when He came to earth.

Jesus opened up Himself so that we could partake in His goodness, His grace, His mercy, and His unfailing love. It gave Jesus great joy to do the work of His Father. His mission was to save and salvage, and to impart wisdom to the world. His mission was founded in God's great love for the world—and Jesus generously gave of Himself in order to facilitate that mission.

One of the most amazing things Jesus ever said about our mission in this life was that we would be able to do the works He did and even greater. Just read the verse for yourself and *think* about it for a moment! *"Verily, verily, I say unto you, He that believeth on Me, the works that I do shall he do also; and greater works than these shall he do; because I go unto My Father"* (John 14:12).

Doing the works of Jesus and greater—that would be total success in my opinion! ALL success takes a backseat to that level of personal success. I mean, just read the works that Jesus did in the Gospels and put yourself in His place. Imagine having the Spirit, the power, and the wisdom to do all that—and then, imagine doing even more. *That's* what Jesus is saying there!

What is the prerequisite for being able to do the works of Christ and more? It's summed up in these five words, *"He that believeth on Me…"* Belief! There is great power in believing on Jesus. What did Jesus do? What His Father, God, led Him to do. In other words, He let the Spirit of God lead Him in His personal life and mission on this planet.

You will not do exactly everything Jesus did, of course—because you have your own personal life and mission, but your mission should always have its foundation in the greater mission of God which is marked by love, joy, peace, and generosity.

Jesus was generous. What God shared with Him, He shares with us—and He wants us to live a life that is similar in that what we've been given, we should freely give to others.

That means you don't have to worry about having "less" when you give to others, and you don't ever have to fall prey to the idea that you are competing with others for anything. You have your own mission, your own place in the scheme of this world, and you can never really "lose" to others when you are following your destiny.

So why not be generous? Why not take as many with you on your way to the top as you can? It's a great principle of success—one that Jesus, through us, is still doing today. We are His hands and we are His feet in this earth.

Jesus Has Taken Us to the Top

God is generous. Jesus knew that was true both in a spiritual way and a financial way. Nowhere in the Bible does it tells us that Jesus ever struggled with the idea that He wouldn't have enough financially—He had faith in God for the finances needed to do what He was called to do.

We don't see Jesus worrying about finances any more than we see Him wringing His hands about how to teach the people. Jesus knew without a shadow of doubt that His heavenly Father would take care of Him and His staff.

Jesus also didn't worry about others recognizing His position. He knew that His Father would exalt Him and exonerate

Him. That's why He told us we could do the same things He could do. He knew without a shadow of doubt that His Father would empower us too!

Again, Jesus was generous and He didn't mind sharing! Jesus chose to take us with Him to the top! That's why Satan hates humanity so much. He tried to go to the top on his own, but couldn't—so he rebelled. God would have exalted him properly for who he was in Heaven, but he couldn't wait. He had to have all the glory for himself. Well, that's not how it works!

As for us, after we sided with the loser and fell from grace, we weren't worthy to go to the top either, but Jesus came and was so generous to us. He chose to die for us, redeem us, and bring us to the top with Him. Heaven after we pass from here, yes, but power and authority to live successfully while we remain here. You see, in the Spirit, once we accept Him, we are seated with Him in heavenly places—and that's high!

Jesus gave us the power to boldly go to the throne of grace. He made us to sit in heavenly places with Him. All we had to do was humble ourselves before Him by acknowledging what He did for us and ask forgiveness for our own sin and *wham*! He exalts us! But He doesn't just take us to a better and higher place in life; Jesus takes us to sit with *Him* in heavenly places. Think about that! There is nothing higher than being side-by-side with the Lord.

Taking on the Spirit of Generosity

In fact, Jesus even goes so far as to call us "His body"—*and* He left us in charge. Now, that is what you call *generous*. Just thinking about that ought to make you shout!

Generosity is at the heart of Christianity. It is the core of redemption—mercy and grace freely and generously given to you and to me. Our job as believers is to take on the spirit of generosity in everything we do.

Generosity not only stimulates success, but it also stimulates joy. If we are successful in an area of our life, it is our responsibility to share that success. It is a joy to pass on what we have learned to others. Why? So that they may learn and grow, and possibly not have to go through what we did to get where we are!

We shouldn't try to make life more difficult for others. We should try to bless others. How do we do that? By giving and sharing what we know—most importantly, by pointing others to the One Who gave us the strength and the grace to succeed.

I Love Being Generous!

I try to be generous as much as I can. People have asked me, "Why do you *want* to be so generous? Most people are looking for what they can get, not what they can give." I've also been asked, "Why do you try to help other preachers get started?" Well the answers are pretty simple—generosity is something I believe is at the heart of Christianity, and I'm commanded to do it. For me, it's about gratitude to God and obedience to His Word. Plus, it just blesses me to do it!

I love being generous. But I think it's impossible to be generous if you have nothing to be generous with—which is one of the reasons I believe in sowing and reaping financially. I believe in the hundred-fold return too, though many don't. But for me, believing and receiving based on Jesus' teaching about the hundred-fold return has given me the ability to be more generous than I ever could have been if I only thought about myself. I love the concept of continual giving and receiving, and giving again!

I know that its God Who puts seed in my hand to sow—and it's His Son's principle of sowing and reaping that I rely upon to keep the blessings flowing. When I pass along these blessings to others, I find that it always warms people's hearts and stimulates them to give and show that kindness to others too. So it's a great cycle that I'm proud to be in.

Generosity breaks down barriers, which is another reason I love being a giver. But again, you can't be a giver if you don't have anything to give. You see, we should always be thinking of others. That's why Jesus said, *"Go ye into all the world, and preach the Gospel to every creature"* (Mark 16:15). That's why He encouraged us to go out and make disciples, not just believers.

Jesus wants you and I to take as many with us to Heaven as we can. And while we're here on earth, He wants us to have what the Word promises—to be blessed in the city and blessed in the field, blessed coming in and blessed going out! Are you getting this? Bring as many with you as you can!

Give Your Time—It's a Precious Commodity

You know, Cathy and I never seem to go on vacation by ourselves. One time we went away to the beach for a long weekend and brought five other couples with us. We had a lot of fun. We rented a place big enough for all of us to have our own bedrooms and we said, "Bring the children too."

It was a busy weekend! They kept saying thank you over and over, and shared how much they appreciated us being generous in taking care of all the expenses. What were Cathy and I doing? We were acting like Jesus, of course. We were living by

His Spirit of genuine generosity. We felt that He would do the same for others.

When I was a little boy, I really loved Christmastime. I loved that all of my cousins were together at Grandma's house. I used to have so much fun. All my uncles and aunts had big families and I liked having all of the people around. I remembered thinking as a boy that, one day, I would go on vacation with a lot of people. Well, on that long weekend at the beach, we had A LOT of people! Ha!

Time is a very precious commodity—and sharing yours with others that you cherish creates some of the most successful moments you will ever have in life. Sharing time, giving of yourself, and having moments that matter to you are important. Make time for those moments!

What You Give Comes Back Multiplied

When you think of others, it is an inspiration from the Holy Spirit. When you give to others, you are acting like the Lord and putting the principle of sowing to work—you are moving the cycle of blessing along. When you pray for others, you are sending waves of love and faith in God toward them. All of these types of things prove that the generous spirit of God lives within you—but more importantly, that you're allowing it to flow.

When you grasp the power in generosity, you will understand that it is a creative force, and it is always, always cycling around the earth. The Word is full of commands to be generous and promises that your generosity will always end up coming back to you. Research for yourself and see.

I love these bits of verses that remind me of the cycle of generosity: *Give and it shall be given unto you* (Luke 6:38); *Cast your bread on the waters for it will find it after many days* (Ecclesiastes 11:1); *Do to others as you would have them do to you* (Luke 6:31); *If someone demands your coat, offer your shirt also* (Luke 6:29); *he who sows bountifully will also reap bountifully* (2 Corinthians 9:6).

There are many more, of course, but the bottom line is that if you are generous and give, you will always find that it comes back to you *multiplied*. And, through your giving, you will inspire others to do the same keeping that cycle of blessing moving throughout the world in obedience to the Lord.

Jesus said that if we had faith the size of a mustard seed, we could throw big mountains into the sea. That is how much power Jesus wanted you to realize that you have. It's big power housed in little faith—and it's *IN* you by the work of the cross.

Mark my words. When you live a life of giving, you will not end up with less. You will have more to give because what you do will be multiplied back to you.

So let the Spirit of generosity flow. Refuse to fear. Wherever you are on your path of success, give of yourself. Don't let it be lonely at the top for you. Take others along with you for the glorious ride. Open up and include others in your life. It's more fun that way and it's the way God intended!

PRINCIPLE
11

Never, Never, Never Report the News— Make the News

God has such a good plan for you and I'm so blessed to share what I've learned in this book. Thank you for reading! It's my prayer that you will prosper in every way—and that you'll be inspired to be who God called you to be and do what He's put on your heart.

Each of these principles have helped me to accomplish goals, complete things that God has led me to do, and to succeed in following His plan for my life—spiritually, physically, and financially. To me, this one is so profound and yet, it's also very simple. This principle can be encapsulated in these words: Never, Never, Never Report the News— Make the News.

Making the News Is About Dominion

God said in the Word that we have dominion over all the works of His hands. So since we have that gift, we have the power to *make* the news, so to speak—and not just report it.

In other words, *you* are in the driver's seat. God has given you the right to forge ahead in life without fear, knowing that you have everything you need by the power of His Spirit to take *dominion* in life and succeed. But you have to know it and use it. Power and dominion are yours—and they are as much a part of who you are as the human body God gave you. When you know who you are, it changes how you act!

In John 7, it describes Jesus going to a feast knowing that He was a wanted man. The officers on duty that day had been given orders to arrest Him, yet they did not do it. You see, there was a lot of public opinion about Jesus. Some believed He was the Christ. Others thought He might just be a deceiver.

Everyone marveled at His miracles, but nobody liked His methods. They hated that He didn't mind healing on the Sabbath. That kind of reaction and fixation on method is called religion! So why didn't the authorities arrest Jesus that day? They had the opportunity. He was right there in front of them.

Jesus told us that it was because His time had not yet come. In other words, He wasn't ready to go yet. The cross was in His future, not in His present. He determined He was not ready to go yet. And the officers didn't do what they were ordered to do.

What did the officers themselves say when they were there with Jesus and yet, not doing their job of arresting Him? The Bible says that when they were questioned by their superiors about why they let Jesus get away, they had only one thing that they could say, "*Never man spake like this man*" (John 7:46).

You see, everyone who heard Jesus that day was affected—even those who were out to do Him harm. Everybody had an opinion. You might say that, on that particular day, Jesus made the news.

Speak with Authority

If you want to be an imitator of Christ and make the *news* instead of just *report* the news, your words must be spoken with authority. You must be able to 1) grasp the truth, 2) use practical forcefulness, and 3) be persuasive.

What you say and how you live must be able to stand up to the world's criticisms because they will have an opinion about you. What gives you the strength to withstand it? God gives it to you! The *passion* for what you believe is, in itself, sustaining. In other words, like Jesus, you've got to *know* that you have the right to be there! You have to *know* that God has put you on earth for a purpose. You will succeed in doing what He's called you to do.

What you *believe* should be the essence of who you *are*—it should emanate out of you. That's how Jesus lived. He believed His Father's message without doubt. He also believed in Himself through and through, so He spoke with authority.

Jesus was a newsmaker! You should be one too. Start strengthening your resolve. Get the Word in you to such a degree that it becomes part of who you *are* and not just what you *believe*.

When you encounter others, apply that truth with practical forcefulness and persuasion. Living like that will lead you to success. Like Jesus, you can be a newsmaker if you will use the power of *authority*.

The Power of the Anointing

Your influence must be greater than public opinion. I call it "the divine effect." The anointing of God is on His Word. When you walk in authority and anointing, it disarms people in every area of their thinking.

When this starts happening, your worth in life to others begins to rise. Doors start opening to you spiritually, physically, and financially. You begin to lead instead of being led. That's why the multitudes followed Christ. He became a newsmaker.

Walking in the anointing of God will naturally cause you to stand out from others, and when you stand out, it's inevitable that people will have an opinion about it. But if you will live with authority and walk in the anointing anyway, you will move ahead with God and become an influence to others.

Refuse to be a slave to public opinion. Choose to succeed anyway.

Doers Have a Message of Hope

To achieve godly success, you must have a message of hope both for yourself and for others. That is so vitally important! Hebrews 11:1 says, *"Now faith is the substance of things hoped for, the evidence of things not seen."*

I've heard it said that hope is like a blueprint. Hope is what faith uses to create what you want. Hope is more than *wanting* change or *wishing* for change. Hope *prepares* our heart to want to change, and to use our faith to make change happen. Are you getting this?

Your life and your words must affect more than just your generation. If Jesus' words revolutionized the thoughts and doctrines of people, I believe yours can too. Again, remember that it was Jesus Who said, *"Verily, verily, I say unto you, he that believeth on Me, the works that I do shall he do also; and greater works than these shall he do; because I go unto My Father"* (John 14:12).

What does that tell you? It tells you that Jesus believes in you! He *wants* you to do great things. He prophesied it over two thousand years ago! We are all connected on this earth, and all of us have a voice. Let yours matter by saying what is good and hopeful!

People never write books about "hearers." They write about doers! That tells you something. In James 1:22, it says, *"But be ye doers of the Word, and not hearers only, deceiving your own selves."* It's sad when you become your own worst enemy, deceiving your own self. Don't let that happen to you. *Do* the Word and believe in yourself.

Refuse to Think Small of Yourself

To make the news instead of just report the news, you must stand out and be outstanding! Now I know that some of you would say to me, "Brother Jesse, I'm shy. I'm not too smart. I'm just a normal person." No, you're not! You are a child of God. You are a giver. You have access to the throne of God. You are the apple of God's eye. Stop selling yourself short!

You are the reason this world exists. God created you to rule and reign, and to do it wonderfully. Never think small! Realize your dominion is powerful and can be used for so much good that your success becomes part of a much larger success.

When you make the news, others will repeat the news, and that means more people will have hope that they too can see the power and dominion in themselves to make their lives, their families, their communities, and the world at large, a much better place to be.

You serve a big God and big things are available to you. Do a study in the Word of who you are "in Christ" and you will be amazed. It will help you to stop thinking small of yourself and start stretching your faith for big things.

You're Not of This World

"Therefore be imitators of God as dear children" (Ephesians 5:1 NKJV). That's a big order, isn't it? But the Word wouldn't say it if *you* couldn't do it. You can! You *are* a newsmaker! I know that may sound too big to you, but it's not.

Out of the billions of people on this earth, God chose *you* as His child and you chose to accept Him as your Father. That's why the world can't understand you. Jesus said it best in John 17:16 when He said, *"They are not of the world, even as I am not of the world."* If we're following Jesus, we are going to stand out. It's just a fact.

Sometimes, what you say to the world may be as deep as a river, but it should never be a muddy river! Your life must be clean and clear. Remember, the only Jesus some people will ever see is the Jesus in you or the Jesus in me.

In Word and Action, LOVE

To make the news instead of report it, you must live a life of love and speak the language of love. The Bible says that love never fails (1 Corinthians 13:8). It also says that faith works *by* love (Galatians 5:6), which means faith won't work *without* love. Love is the best tasting fruit of the Spirit. The love of God for people is the reason I preach this gospel:

For God so loved the world, that He gave His only begotten Son, that whosoever believeth in Him should not perish, but have everlasting life.

For God sent not His Son into the world to condemn the world; but that the world through Him might be saved.

John 3:16-17

Love what God loves—people. Use your dominion—not to crush, but to succeed in lifting people up. Use your dominion to steer your own life and spread the love of God so others can see what hope and faith are too.

Don't waste your dominion on foolish things like hatred, anger, revenge, competition, spite or any of those things that only bring cruelty and corruption. And by all means, don't waste your breath reporting the bad news of others!

God has given you a mission to spread the Good News! So, make your life, your success, and your words something that stand out in the mud and muck of this world's darkness.

When you speak, make it count. When you act, act right. When you wake up in the morning and with every decision you make, realize that God has given YOU dominion. This is your life. Don't waste it and report everybody else's news. Do what you are meant to do. Go out there into the world and make some news!

PRINCIPLE
12

Never Waste Your Energy and Zeal On Projects That Don't Work

Whatever big idea you have, before you make the choice to go full steam ahead toward it, you must decide within yourself that the idea is more than just a *good* idea—it must be a *God* idea.

A good idea is a fifty/fifty proposition. You have no clue if it will work. Because if you have a good idea but you don't know that God is in it, you won't have the faith or confidence you need to see it to completion. Ideas take work and I've found, as a believer, that there is little joy in ideas that God is not behind. I need full faith in an idea to see it to completion—I need to know that it's more than a good idea. It must be a God-idea!

A God-idea is one that you've consulted the Lord about and gotten the "go-ahead." That's the kind of idea that will create energy and cause creative juices to start flowing in others, even in sinners. It's a project that will work! You can be more passionate, more resilient and more dedicated when you are dealing with a God-idea than you ever can if you're just working on a good idea.

The Tower of Babel Was a "Good Idea"

People can drum up their own energy and get a lot done—but it won't end up joyful and it won't create success that lasts. In fact, God Himself will sometimes intervene to make sure it doesn't! The Tower of Babel is a good example of that.

As you read this story in Genesis, you'll see that it happened *after* the flood of Noah. People were united about that tower. They wanted longevity—to make a name for themselves and show the world what they could do.

In fact, it seemed like all of mankind suddenly had this innate feeling that the secret to success was focused unity, and they were right! Even God acknowledged that they had the power to succeed.

What was wrong with their tower idea? It wasn't a God-idea! They'd already forgotten the lesson from the flood that, when you put yourself ahead of God, trouble is going to come.

In Genesis 11:4, they said, *"Let us make us a name, lest we be scattered abroad upon the face of the whole earth."* Notice they had an idea, but they didn't pray about it. They didn't ask God what He thought of their idea. They figured that they could do it by themselves. So they began to try.

You see, that's the problem with a good idea instead of a God-idea:

The minute you cut God out, you begin to lose energy and zeal. The favor from God begins to cease and obstacles begin to get bigger.

Obedience Brings Godly Success

The Tower of Babel was a great idea, but because it wasn't a God-idea, it ended up being a waste of energy and zeal. You may have a good idea, but again I ask you, is it a God-idea?

When I began this ministry in 1978, I made up my mind that no matter how good something sounded, I would go to God for direction. In Psalm 34:10, it says, *"The young lions do lack, and suffer hunger: but they that seek the Lord shall not want any good thing."* I have proven that many times over and over in my ministry because God has been involved in the decisions.

You see, I realized years ago that I did not want to waste energy and zeal on something that God said not to do. There is just no point in leaving God out—and no fear in approaching God about anything—so why leave Him out? Our success is so much sweeter when we are at peace knowing God is with us every step of the way.

It doesn't matter if everybody else is on board, God must be first for all things to work together for good!

Don't Waste Your Time Consult God FIRST

John 10:4-5 tells us that His sheep know His voice and a stranger they will not follow. If you get an idea and you think it's a good one, I encourage you to please consult the Lord about it.

Recognize God's authority. Honor Him by making Him the first one you consult with. Don't fear what the Lord may say—be excited that you have Him to turn to and help you. You need His direction, I promise you.

So let God be the One to speak *first* concerning your future. You should speak *second*. A good idea may have come from Him. He may have dropped it into your spirit. If so, let Him speak to you about it more. Never just charge ahead without His approval in prayer.

I've seen so many people waste their energy and time on things God never told them to do—they drain themselves for future successes by wasting time with ideas they never bothered to consult with God about.

Fear Is the Opposite of Faith—Maintain Your Spiritual Focus

If you spiritually drain yourself, you will open yourself up to failure. From that failure, more apprehension and fear is produced in your mind—and the buildup of fear will create an atmosphere inside you that will inhibit your success.

What is fear? Fear is the opposite of faith—and it is a tangible reminder that you are lacking spiritual strength. The joy of the Lord is your strength. Fear robs you of it.

When you hit a buildup of fear, you must tear it down by building up your faith with the word of God. You must realign your spirit with God's Spirit by refocusing what you are allowing to rule your mind. The fruit of the Spirit will follow suit.

Love must become a focus because God is love, and when you are dealing with fear, you must realize God has made you worthy through His Son. You are worth the effort of fulfilling His plan for your life. You have what it takes to do what He said, and have what He said you could have. Nothing is impossible to them who believe. God wants the best for you and has created you to succeed, but your best and most lasting success in life will always come when you do things His way.

Your best ideas will come from Him. Your greatest faith and tenacity to fulfill those ideas will come when you pursue not only the idea, but also Him. Putting God first is an all-inclusive principle for success.

God-ideas are hard work, but they are good work! Never be afraid of the work! It takes work to be successful in anything. When you love it, it may not always feel like work but believe me, you are working nevertheless—and you are working for something good.

While success comes many different ways and it looks different to different people, if God is in your heart and you are following His lead, the success that you are looking for will come. No matter what you need to get there, it will be provided. No matter what comes up to get you off track, He will help you to either overcome it or move it right out of your way.

Whatever your goal, mission, or heart's desire—never forget that before it ever landed into your heart, it was in God's heart first. So have faith in God. Trust the God that trusts in you. He has all the wisdom, guidance, and power to get you where you need to be and when you need to be there! The steps of a good man are ordered by the Lord, and I know that you will see great success as you walk with Him!

The Ribbon That Ties All 12 Principles Together

Well this is the end of the book, and I hope you've enjoyed it! Every one of these 12 Principles for Success have helped me tremendously in my life and ministry. Except for this last principle, I listed them in no particular order because each has been a lesson for me unto itself. But the point of Principle 12 is listed last because it really is the ribbon that ties them all together—and it can be summed up in three words:

Obedience to God

When Jesus went to the cross, He gave His life for you and for me and for the whole world. His sacrifice redeemed us and gave us unblocked access to the Father. So now, no matter what our destiny, we can be sure that God is with us, God is listening, and God is available to help us as we make our way to success.

Through God's Word and the still, small voice that He's put in our heart, we can be sure that obeying Him has never been easier or more rewarding. We are His children and because of that, His anointing is on us to do what He has dropped into our hearts to do!

Work is part of it and with success you sometimes also get persecution from the enemy too, but don't let that deter you. Just stay close to the Lord and move forward anyway. Life isn't always easy but God created us to live it! To overcome! To move mountains. To "fight the good fight of faith" and win! Because we have Him, we can run the race that is set before us, finish our course, and enter into His rest with a smile on our face knowing we did all we could do to fulfill His good plan for our life!

So, run your race well. Always consult the Lord and always obey. It's the greatest secret to your success. If you consult Him, stick with Him, stay passionate about Him, and follow His lead, doors will open that you *never* imagined possible.

God bless you as you go and do what He alone has put on your heart!

About the Author

Jesse Duplantis is a dynamic evangelist who has traveled throughout the world since 1978 preaching the Gospel of Jesus Christ. He is the founder of Jesse Duplantis Ministries (JDM), which, since its inception, has been using every available voice to invade the earth with God's love. JDM has its International Headquarters in Destrehan, Louisiana and additional offices in the United Kingdom and Australia.

A favorite program for many seeking to know more about God, Jesse Duplantis' weekly television program has grown miraculously over the years and is reaching 2.7 billion potential viewers worldwide—302 million in the USA alone. Jesse believes that TV is an incredible tool for the Lord Jesus Christ and he is seizing every opportunity available to use it to populate Heaven. His television broadcast is aired in 255 countries and via satellite reaches every inch of planet earth. Jesse says, "We are redefining the word broadcast to mean every way we can broadcast our weekly program throughout the earth through TV, Internet, Social Media, and even more to come."

In 1997, he and his wife, the Reverend Cathy Duplantis, founded Covenant Church, the International Headquarters Church of Jesse Duplantis Ministries in Destrehan, Louisiana, a suburb in the Greater New Orleans area. In recognition of his many years of effectively sharing God's message of salvation through Jesus Christ to the world, Jesse Duplantis was awarded an honorary doctorate of divinity degree from Oral Roberts University in 1999.

Today, Jesse Duplantis is one of the most unique and beloved ministers of our generation. He not only shares his memorable mix of strong, biblical preaching and hilarious life lessons through his television program, but also through evangelistic meetings in churches and convention centers, local church outreaches, books that have been translated in many languages, magazines, the Internet, social media, and his many inspirational audio/visual teaching resources. Jesse Duplantis is spreading the Gospel of Jesus in a way that is reaching people and changing lives, one soul at a time.

Known throughout the world for his joy and his exuberant, evangelistic spirit, Jesse Duplantis is often told that he is "the only preacher my husband and kids will listen to!" Why is that? It's not just because "Jesse is funny," and it's not just because "Jesse is real." People listen because Jesse Duplantis is a true evangelist and revivalist. It's the anointing of Jesus Christ on the evangelist to reach the "unreachable," and it's the anointing of Jesus Christ on the revivalist to rekindle the fire in believers. People listen because they need the anointing of Jesus—and Jesus is the message that Jesse Duplantis preaches.

For more than 39 years now, Jesse Duplantis has had one vision, one goal and one mission: World Evangelism. It is his mission to reach every soul of the 7 billion people that now inhabit the earth, making sure that each one has an opportunity to know the *real* Jesus—approachable, personable, compassionate, and full of joy—the way that he knows Jesus.

PRAYER OF SALVATION

God loves you—no matter who you are, no matter what your past. God loves you so much that He gave His one and only begotten Son for you. The Bible tells us that "...whoever believes in Him shall not perish but have eternal life" (John 3:16 NIV). Jesus laid down His life and rose again so that we could spend eternity with Him in heaven and experience His absolute best on earth. If you would like to receive Jesus into your life, say the following prayer out loud and mean it from your heart.

Heavenly Father, I come to You admitting that I am a sinner. Right now, I choose to turn away from sin, and I ask You to cleanse me of all unrighteousness. I believe that Your Son, Jesus, died on the cross to take away my sins. I also believe that He rose again from the dead so that I might be forgiven of my sins and made righteous through faith in Him. I call upon the name of Jesus Christ to be the Savior and Lord of my life. Jesus, I choose to follow You and ask that You fill me with the power of the Holy Spirit. I declare that right now I am a child of God. I am free from sin and full of the righteousness of God. I am saved in Jesus' name. Amen.

If you prayed this prayer to receive Jesus Christ as your Savior for the first time, please contact us on the Web at **www.harrisonhouse.com** to receive a free book.

Or you may write to us at
Harrison House • P.O. Box 35035 • Tulsa, Oklahoma 74153

The Harrison House Vision

Proclaiming the truth and the power

Of the Gospel of Jesus Christ

With excellence;

Challenging Christians to

Live victoriously,

Grow spiritually,

Know God intimately.

Fast. Easy.
Convenient.

For the latest Harrison House product information and author news, look no further than your computer. All the details on our powerful, life-changing products are just a click away. New releases, e-mail subscriptions, testimonies, monthly specials — find it all in one place. Visit **harrison**house.com today!

harrisonhouse.com